CW01655746

In My *Healing* Era

JACLYN DUNNE

BALBOA.PRESS
A DIVISION OF HAY HOUSE

Copyright © 2025 Jaclyn Dunne.

All rights reserved. No part of this book may be used or reproduced by any means, graphic, electronic, or mechanical, including photocopying, recording, taping or by any information storage retrieval system without the written permission of the author except in the case of brief quotations embodied in critical articles and reviews.

Balboa Press books may be ordered through booksellers or by contacting:

Balboa Press
A Division of Hay House
1663 Liberty Drive
Bloomington, IN 47403
www.balboapress.co.uk
UK TFN: 0800 0148647 (Toll Free inside the UK)
UK Local: (02) 0369 56325 (+44 20 3695 6325 from outside the UK)

Because of the dynamic nature of the Internet, any web addresses or links contained in this book may have changed since publication and may no longer be valid. The views expressed in this work are solely those of the author and do not necessarily reflect the views of the publisher, and the publisher hereby disclaims any responsibility for them.

The author of this book does not dispense medical advice or prescribe the use of any technique as a form of treatment for physical, emotional, or medical problems without the advice of a physician, either directly or indirectly. The intent of the author is only to offer information of a general nature to help you in your quest for emotional and spiritual well-being. In the event you use any of the information in this book for yourself, which is your constitutional right, the author and the publisher assume no responsibility for your actions.

Any people depicted in stock imagery provided by Getty Images are models, and such images are being used for illustrative purposes only. Certain stock imagery © Getty Images.

Print information available on the last page.

ISBN: 979-8-7652-1618-7 (sc)
ISBN: 979-8-7652-1619-4 (e)

Library of Congress Control Number: 2025924652

Balboa Press rev. date: 11/20/2025

For Angelica and Honey, I hope I have inspired
you to walk boldly where no map is drawn.
Unpredictable paths lead to unexpected treasure.

Contents

Chapter 3: Peace

Prologue

My healing era didn't begin abruptly. There was no health scare, job loss or empty nest. There was no big moment or realisation, more a series of nudges that invited change. The irony is, this slow, quiet realisation prompted a series of big life changes including an emotional low, the end of my 16-year marriage which meant a new home and business too.

What began as a feeling of unease, progressed over a 10-year period to intense inner turmoil which I could no longer distract myself from. I tried for so long to suppress my feelings as I knew facing them, voicing them and acting upon them would cause a cataclysmic event for my loved ones.

I'm sure there are many people (and not just women) who can resonate with suppressing their own feelings and needs because they believe they have a responsibility to keep the peace, not to disrupt or cause inconvenience to others. This is personified when you can't even truly pinpoint exactly why you feel so unhappy. From the outside looking in, you have it all, a loving husband, incredible children, a beautiful home and a successful business. Every day, you wake up and role play this 'perfect' life, but you can't shake the feeling. You tell no-one because the first thing they would ask is "why aren't you happy?' and you wouldn't be able to answer with any clarity. So, you suppress, you carry on, you tell yourself to stop being silly, to just get on with it, but the feelings get stronger, and the internal noise gets louder.

Feeling broken is a hopeless sentiment, feeling broken in silence is desolate.

Emotions are eventually verbalised, first you may start to drop hints thinking it will be enough, subtle remarks slowly become emotional disconnection when they fall on deaf ears and before you know it years have passed where you no longer recognise yourself. You are a version of a person people expect you to be, but it feels so unaligned, so forced, so inauthentic. These were the nudges that invited change and so begun my healing era.

There doesn't have to be a seismic event for a healing era to begin, but take heed, once the quiet aches for change are honoured, healing may just cause a seismic event to take place!! This has certainly been my experience although I'm sure each emotional healing journey will be completely individual, just as physical healing is.

Finally listening to my inner cries for change was initially met with much pain. Reality can be painful, but it shouldn't be ignored. Once you are brave enough to confront your feelings, you are also creating space to process them and journey back to peace.

If you read my first book Mind Body Miracle, published in 2017, you will know I have used journaling, not only as a method of introspection but to increase self-awareness, emotional processing and clarity of thought. Journaling has scientifically backed benefits from reducing stress and anxiety to faster physical healing, according to a 2013 study in Psychosomatic Medicine.

What started as the ramblings of a mad woman (which was very nearly the title of this book) fast become daily documenting of my transition from pain, through processing and into peace: my healing Era. Healing is never linear, whether mental, emotional, physical or spiritual, it's not a predictable journey from bad to better. Instead, it's messy, cyclical and full of unexpected setbacks where you may be forced to visit old emotions and triggers, but with each cycle a deeper understanding is often gained, moving us closer to a healed response each time.

I had absolutely no intention of sharing my journal entries with a wider audience but as the processing began, I found the courage to share them with close friends who found my words inspiring and gave me the confidence to publish them. My hope is you too will find comfort and inspiration in these pages. Whether you are feeling alone, unsupported, suffering, processing or in your very own healing era may my words echo in your mind and serve as a gentle prompt that you do not walk this path alone. May your boundaries become unapologetically strong, may you crave quiet more than chaos, may you respond and not react, and may your circle be full of kindness and understanding as opposed to drama and gossip, above all may you become the version of yourself you feel most at peace with.

Let the Healing Era commence.

CHAPTER ONE

Pain

Letting Go

Letting go of what is familiar, even when it feels safe, even when it has cradled you in moments of fear or uncertainty is one of the hardest acts of courage. But safety and growth rarely share the same space.

The comfort zone, while soothing, is often a quiet cage that keeps your potential at bay. True evolution asks you to step into the unknown, to release the habits, people, roles, and versions of yourself that no longer align with who you're becoming. It's not a betrayal of the past, but an honouring of your capacity to expand beyond it.

Stagnation might feel easier, but it slowly dulls the spirit. Growth, though uncertain and sometimes painful, is where vitality lives. You are not meant to remain unchanged, you are meant to rise, to stretch, to evolve into the deeper truth of who you are. Letting go is not a loss; it is a passage.

To let go is not just to release, but to trust, trust that life has something greater waiting beyond what you can currently see. It's a surrendering of control, of needing to know every step before it's taken. And in that surrender, there is a quiet power: the willingness to allow life to unfold in its own time, in its own way.

Allowing means softening your grip and making space for what is meant for you to arrive, often unexpectedly, but always with purpose.

It's in this trusting, this sacred allowing, that transformation truly begins.

Beautifully Broken

There is a rare kind of beauty in being broken, not in the way things shatter and are discarded, but in the way a soul fractures and still chooses to shine through the cracks.

To be beautifully broken is to wear your scars like scripture, evidence of pain survived, lessons learned, and truths unearthed. It is to recognise that perfection is a myth, and that real strength lives in vulnerability, in the trembling voice that still speaks, the tired heart that still loves.

Being imperfectly perfect means embracing the chaos and grace within you, understanding that every flaw and wrinkle tells a story worth hearing.

Weathered and wise, you become a mosaic of moments, some joyful, some devastating, but all necessary, all sacred. And in that acceptance, there is peace: not in being whole, but in being wholly, unapologetically human; a human who is journeying through life and becoming stronger in body, softer in heart and sharper in mind, finally in acceptance of me!

Loss and Light

Losing someone close feels like having a part of yourself suddenly torn away, leaving behind a silence that echoes louder than any sound. It's as if the world keeps moving, but you're standing still, unable to find your footing in a place that no longer feels the same. Their absence leaves a void so deep it's hard to breathe sometimes, and you find yourself searching for them in memories, in dreams, in everyday moments where they should still be.

Grief wraps itself around you like a fog, blurring everything, and you're left not just mourning their loss, but the loss of who you were with them, feeling lost in a life that now feels unfamiliar.

Sometimes in the stillness that follows their absence, a deeper ache begins to surface, not just the pain of losing them, but the unsettling question of whether their presence had been the only thing anchoring you.

You wonder if the feeling of being lost began with their death, or if, in truth, you'd been adrift long before, and their love, their laughter, their constant presence had simply kept you from noticing it.

It's a disorienting thought, that maybe they didn't just leave a void but revealed one that was already there. And now, in their absence, you're left to face not only the weight of grief, but the quiet, haunting question of who you are without them, and who you were all along.

So now you're left with the hardest question of all: how do I find myself? In the quiet after loss, when everything feels fractured and unfamiliar, the search for yourself can feel overwhelming, like trying to piece together a puzzle when you're not even sure what the picture is supposed to be.

You wonder where to begin, or if there's even a version of you that exists outside of who you were with them. But maybe finding yourself isn't about having clear answers or sudden clarity. Maybe it's about sitting with the pain without rushing to escape it, gently exploring the parts of you that remain, and letting yourself grow slowly from the inside out.

It might take time.

It might feel messy and uncertain.

But perhaps that's okay, because becoming isn't a destination. It's a quiet, ongoing act of remembering who you are beneath the sorrow, and learning, day by day, how to live with both the loss and the light still flickering within you.

I Choose Me (and that's not selfish)!

Today, I reminded myself of something difficult, but necessary: It's okay to walk away from love that no longer feels like home. I used to think that once you chose someone, once you built a life, made promises, prayed for forever, that leaving meant failure. That it meant giving up. But now I'm beginning to understand staying in a love that no longer nurtures your soul is a quieter kind of abandonment. One you do to yourself.

And I don't want to keep abandoning myself.

I've been holding this weight in my chest for a while now, this quiet ache that whispered, *"This isn't how I want to be loved, not for the rest of my life."* And I ignored it. I tried to be grateful. I tried to convince myself that maybe this was just what love looked like after the early magic wore off.

But deep down, I knew love shouldn't feel like silence between two people who used to be each other's home. It shouldn't feel like shrinking to fit or softening your truth just to keep the peace.

Sometimes, you outgrow the very thing you once begged the universe for. And that's the hardest part. To admit that your heart has changed, even when the memory of how it once beat for them still lingers.

I won't lie to myself: I'm scared. There are nights when the quiet is so loud it feels unbearable. I question my choice. I imagine a hundred other versions of us, ones where we made it, where I didn't have to choose between them and myself. But none of those imagined versions fix the truth: that the way they love me is not the way I need to be loved.

And that's not selfish. It's just real.

I can still care for someone and accept that we are no longer right for each other. I can still feel love and choose to leave. That contradiction used to paralyze me, but now I see it for what it is: a kind of strength. A kind of honesty. A decision to stop bleeding for something just because it once made me feel alive.

So, I will let myself grieve. I will let the ache come, the questions come, the what-ifs come. And when they do, I will hold myself gently and remind myself why I chose to go: because I deserve a love that feels like peace, like clarity, like home, not just in the beginning, but every day.

I don't know what the future holds. But I know this: I'm no longer willing to settle for anything less than a love that meets me where I am and walks with me toward who I'm becoming. And that, that feels like the beginning of something honest.

The version they never knew

I spoke in truth,
you heard a ghost,
a version drawn
from fears you host.
I stood in light,
but through your shade,
you painted me
from stories made.
You knew the shell,
not what was deep,
the thoughts I held,
the wounds I keep.
I grieve the space
you never saw,
the quiet heart,
the inner law
But when peace comes,
not dressed in rage,
it turns the page,
and leaves the cage.
I don't need proof
to just be me,
no mirror cracked
can set me free.
So, walk your road
with your belief,
I'll walk in mine,
and find relief.

The Dark Night of the Soul

There are moments when the soul feels stripped bare, when the noise of the world fades, and all you're left with is silence and shadow.

This is not a failure, nor a punishment. It is a sacred turning, a passage through fire. In this darkness, your illusions fall away, and though it feels like unravelling, it is, in truth, becoming.

You are meeting yourself beyond titles, beyond expectations, meeting the raw, unedited truth of who you are. Trust that even in this void, something powerful is happening. You are not lost. You are being remade.

There are times in life when everything familiar burns away, when you stand in the ashes of what was, unsure if anything true will rise. This is the dark night of the soul, where the fire is not here to destroy you, but to refine you. It burns away what you no longer need; old beliefs, worn-out identities, quiet lies you told yourself to survive. Though it feels like breaking, it is in fact the slow and sacred art of becoming. You are walking through fire, yes, but you are also being forged by it. And when the dawn returns, as it always does, you will not be the same. You will be something stronger yet softer. Something born of flame, but no longer afraid of it

It strips you of what you thought you were, of all whom can no longer walk with you. And though it feels like ruin, it is a sacred unravelling. You are not breaking; you are being broken open. In the ashes of what was, the first breath of who you are becoming begins. Rebirth does not arrive gently, it rises from flame, from surrender, from courage you didn't know you had.

When you emerge, you will not be who you were. You will be something wiser, wilder, more whole, reborn not despite the fire, but because of it.

Lost and Found

Rejection and abandonment cut deeply because they strike at our longing to belong, to be seen to matter.

When we are left behind or turned away, it can feel as though the ground beneath us has shifted, leaving us unmoored, uncertain of who we are without the reflection of another's acceptance.

But in that aching silence, after the door closes, after the final word is spoken, there is an invitation to meet ourselves more honestly.

Feeling lost is not the end, but the beginning of a journey inward, where we learn that our worth was never dependent on being chosen, and our path was never meant to be lit by someone else's approval.

In time, the absence becomes space, the pain becomes clarity, and we begin to rebuild not from what we've lost, but from what we've discovered within.

The Pedestal and the Fall

One of the hardest lessons in life is learning that people are not who we imagine them to be.

We meet someone, perhaps they inspire us, offer comfort, or seem to carry a rare light and we place them high on a pedestal built from our hopes, ideals, and admiration. We believe in their perfection, in their unwavering goodness. We invest parts of ourselves in who we want them to be, often blind to the truth of who they really are.

But people are not pedestals. They are human; flawed, complex, sometimes selfish, sometimes lost themselves.

When they falter, when they fall short, the crash is deafening, not just for them, but for us. Because what shatters isn't just the illusion of them, but the version of ourselves that believed we were safe in their hands.

The lesson is brutal: not everyone deserves the pedestal we place them on. Sometimes, love or admiration doesn't mean they can carry the weight of our expectations.

But this pain, as sharp as it is, teaches us discernment.

To love people for who they are, not who we need them to be.

To hold others in kindness, not in worship.

And most importantly, to reserve that highest pedestal for ourself, because we are the ones who must carry our hearts through the disappointment, stand when others fall, and rise when illusions crumble.

I am crossing

I didn't choose for the ground to change,
but here I am
barefoot on the edge of what was,
the air thick with goodbye.
I can still hear the rhythm of my old life
beating softly behind me,
calling me back with its quiet certainty,
but I know that door
no longer opens for me.

Ahead, there is only mist.
I can't see where my next step will land,
but I can feel my heart
urging me forward
a whisper I almost trust.
In one palm, I hold the ache
for what I've lost.
In the other,
a fragile pulse of hope.

They weigh differently each day,
I am learning to walk like this
not waiting to be ready,
not waiting to be sure
just placing one foot,
then the next,
until the unknown
starts to know me back.

The Mask Slips

Sometimes the hardest truth to carry is the one no one else sees, the quiet certainty that someone adored by many is not who they pretend to be. It's a lonely kind of knowing, when the world applauds their charm, kindness, or success, while you've witnessed the shadows they carefully hide.

You first start to question your own clarity, wondering if you're too harsh, too sensitive, too unforgiving. But deep down, there's a knowing, a subtle fracture in their mask you've seen too many times to ignore. In that space, between who they appear to be and who they truly are, you stand silently, holding a truth no one else is ready to hear.

Every mask slips eventually, no matter how carefully it's crafted or convincingly worn. Time has a way of revealing what intention tries to hide, peeling back the layers of charm, generosity, or innocence to expose the motives beneath.

It might not happen loudly or all at once; sometimes it's in the smallest cracks, a moment of weakness or anger, caught off guard, a lie told too easily, a truth twisted just enough.

When it happens, when the illusion breaks, those who once praised them are left stunned, while you, who saw it all along, are left with the quiet ache of being right.

CHAPTER TWO

Processing

Live Deliberately

To live deliberately is to move through life with intention rather than inertia, to stop sleepwalking through your days and start choosing them with awareness and purpose.

It means asking yourself not just *what* you're doing, but *why:* why you say yes to certain things, why you stay in places or relationships that drain you, why you postpone what truly matters.

Living deliberately is about stripping away the noise and tuning into the quiet truth of what aligns with your values, your soul, your one brief, sacred life. It's in the courage to slow down in a world obsessed with speed, to say no when you mean it, to savour moments rather than collect them like trophies. It's choosing depth over distraction, presence over performance, and connection over convenience.

To live deliberately is not always easy, but it is always honest, and in that honesty, we may find freedom.

Trusting My Inner Voice

There is a quiet knowing inside me, a voice that whispers truths before logic catches up.
For too long, I've brushed it aside, measuring my choices against the expectations of others, seeking approval instead of alignment. But I'm beginning to see the cost of that.

Every time I silence my intuition in favour of someone else's opinion, I feel a little more disconnected from myself.

Their voices get louder, whilst mine gets dimmer.

Eventually, I forget what my own truth even sounds like.

Today, I choose to come home to myself.

To sit with that subtle, sacred voice that rises from within, even if it goes against the grain.
Even if it makes others uncomfortable.
Even if it leads me somewhere unfamiliar.

Because intuition doesn't always give me a full map, just the next step. But when I follow it, I feel whole. I feel rooted. I feel real.

That is a feeling no external validation can replace. From this place, everything begins to change: my decisions carry weight, not because they're approved by others, but because they're true for me.

I stop performing. I start living.

The people who are meant to walk with me, they don't need me to shrink or bend. They just need me to be honest.

So here I am:

Choosing to listen within.
Choosing to lead with trust.
Choosing, finally, to value my intuition over the noise.

Learning to Love Yourself

Learning to love yourself begins the moment you decide to become your own best friend. It's choosing to stand by yourself with the same loyalty, patience, and kindness you've given to others, especially when the world feels unkind or when your inner critic grows loud.

Loving yourself means recognizing your worth not because of what you've done or how you look, but simply because you exist. It's whispering words of encouragement to yourself in the silence, holding space for your pain without judgment, and celebrating your smallest victories like they matter, because they do.

Being your own best friend is not about isolation but about knowing that no matter who walks away or what life throws your way, you will not abandon yourself. It is the most intimate and transformative relationship you will ever build and the foundation for all the others.

Learning to love yourself is a journey that demands both courage and compassion, a quiet, often messy rebellion against every voice, internal or external, that ever told you that you weren't enough. It's not about perfection or endless self-affirmation, but about meeting yourself in the mirror, scars, flaws, and all, and choosing to be kind anyway.

It's the radical act of accepting your past without letting it define your worth, and embracing your body, your voice, your soul, even on the days they feel heavy.

Loving yourself means reclaiming your power, not through grand gestures, but in the gentle, persistent decision to treat yourself with the same tenderness you've offered others so freely. It's deep work. Sacred work.

It changes everything.

To Whom It May Concern

I'm truly sorry for the ways I've let my pain spill onto you, for bleeding on you through wounds you never caused.

Sometimes, the hurt I carry from the past leaks out as distance or silence, and it's unfair that you've had to feel the weight of emotions that were never yours to bear.

You didn't inflict these wounds, yet you've felt their sting through me.

Please know that my actions weren't a reflection of your worth, but a reflection of my own unresolved hurt. I am working on healing, not just for myself, but so I can be the kind of presence that brings peace, not pain. Thank you for your patience, I hope you can forgive me for the times I've made you carry what was mine to hold.

I am a work in progress, still learning how to hold and process hurt without letting it spill onto others, still unlearning the patterns that pain has etched into me. Healing isn't linear and some days I fall short, not because I don't care, but because I'm still finding my way.

I'm trying to become more aware, more responsible for the energy I bring into the spaces we share. Please know that every step I take, no matter how small, is with the hope of showing up better, more present, more whole.

I may not be there yet, but I am committed to the journey, and I'm grateful for your grace as I walk it.

Unshakeable

There comes a moment when pain, once silently endured, transforms into anger.

Not the kind that consumes, but the kind that clarifies.

It's the fire that burns away weakness and lights the path to strength.

Hurt teaches humility, but anger demands change.

It's the voice of the wounded saying, "No more."

When you've been betrayed, dismissed, or broken, let the anger remind you that you deserve better, not just from others, but from yourself.

Forgive, not to let them off the hook, but to release yourself from the chains of bitterness.

But never forget.

Let the memory shape your boundaries, sharpen your vision, and fuel your rise.

Your scars are not signs of defeat; they are symbols of survival.

Use them.

Build from them.

Become unshakable.

It Was Never My Job to Fix It

Today, this truth hit me with unexpected force: *It was never my job to fix it.*

Not the broken dynamics.
Not someone else's anger.
Not the silence in the room.

For so long, I believed that if I just tried harder, stayed quieter, or gave more of myself, things would finally feel okay, not just for me, but for everyone else. But I'm beginning to see that I was never supposed to be the fixer.

I just didn't know any other way to feel safe or needed.
I carried other people's pain as if it were my own.
I made excuses for behaviour that hurt me.
I convinced myself that love meant sacrifice, even when that sacrifice cost me pieces of who I am.

None of that was ever truly my responsibility. It wasn't mine to hold and it wasn't mine to heal. I'm learning now that letting go is an act of love, not just for others, but for myself.

I don't have to carry what was never mine. I can feel the grief of that, honour the effort I gave, and still choose to return to myself.

My job was never to fix them.
My job is to be true to me.

Unapologetically Worthy

We often chase external validation as if it were the key to our worth, longing for approval, applause, or affirmation to feel enough. But the truth is, anything rooted outside of us can be taken, changed, or withheld. When we anchor our value in others' perceptions, we give them quiet control over our self-esteem.

Yet, self-validation, honouring our truth, trusting our inner voice, and recognising our inherent worth creates a foundation no one can shake. It's not arrogance; it's liberation. When we learn to affirm ourselves from within, we no longer need to beg the world to tell us we matter, we already know.

When we truly know ourselves, we begin to understand that we were never meant to compete, we were meant to contribute. In a world that constantly compares, we forget that our uniqueness is not a flaw to fix but a gift to offer. There is no one else with our exact blend of experiences, voice, perspective, or heart.

When we validate ourselves from within, we no longer feel the urge to outshine others just to feel seen. We realise we are already enough, not because we've achieved more, looked better, or pleased everyone, but because our worth was never conditional to begin with.

From that place of inner knowing, life stops being a race and becomes a space where we can show up fully, authentically, and without apology.

The Tide of Time

Time breathes differently when you're processing change, its rhythm no longer steady, but staggered, stretched, and compressed in strange ways. Moments that once passed unnoticed now hang heavy with significance, and days can feel like lifetimes as your mind replays what was and grapples with what might be.

In the heart of transition, the present feels blurred, suspended between the echo of the past and the uncertainty of what's coming. Time, once a reliable current, becomes a tide, sometimes pulling you back into memory, sometimes thrusting you forward with urgency.

Change alters perception, and in that altered state, even the ticking of a clock can feel unfamiliar, as if the universe itself is pausing to let you catch your breath.

Courageously surrender to the transition, be willing to release the illusion of control, the dictation of time and instead let the unfamiliar shape you. It is in this surrender that transformation begins, not by force, but through a soft unfolding. When you stop resisting, you create space for clarity to emerge from the fog, and for strength to rise from stillness.

The discomfort doesn't vanish, but it becomes bearable, even meaningful, when you stop trying to rush through it.

You begin to understand that this in-between space, however raw or uncertain, is sacred ground, where old selves are shed, and new ones gently begin to form.

In the Absence of an Apology

Letting go of the need for an apology is one of the most liberating acts of self-respect.

It means releasing yourself from the grip of someone else's inability to take responsibility and choosing peace over the weight of expectation. It's not about pretending the hurt didn't happen, it's about acknowledging that your healing cannot be held hostage by someone else's silence or denial.

You make peace not because they made it right, but because you deserve freedom from the ache of waiting. In that quiet surrender, you reclaim your power, your dignity, and your right to move forward, whole and unburdened.

The absence of an apology is not a reflection of your worth, but a revealing glimpse into theirs. It does not mean your pain was invalid or that your experience was imagined, it simply shows the limitations of the other person's emotional maturity, courage, or compassion. Their silence speaks not to your value, but to their inability to confront truth or offer accountability.

You are not unworthy of acknowledgment; they are unready or unwilling to give it,
and that distinction matters deeply because it reminds you that your healing isn't proof of their remorse, but of your resilience.

Trigger Happy

Another trigger arrives, unexpected but familiar, and suddenly the past is no longer past, it's present, raw, and loud. Healing childhood wounds isn't a straight path; it's a spiral, bringing you back to the same ache until you can meet it with softer eyes.

Each trigger is a painful messenger, not a punishment, a reminder of the parts of you still longing to be seen, heard, and held with compassion.

As hard as it is, this moment is sacred.

It's a chance to sit with the younger version of yourself who never felt safe, who learned to shrink or shout or hide to survive. Now, as the adult, you can choose differently. You can offer yourself the gentleness and care that were missing. Healing isn't forgetting or fixing the past, it's learning how to love yourself through the echoes of it.

Healing is not pretty, it's messy, uncomfortable, and often lonely. It looks like crying over things you thought you were 'over', setting boundaries that make people uncomfortable, and sitting with feelings that don't have easy answers. It means confronting truths you once buried just to make it through.

There's nothing glamorous about facing the parts of yourself you were taught to hide.

But it's worth it.

Every painful step is a movement towards freedom, a chance to break patterns, to breathe without the weight of old stories, to live from a place of truth rather than survival.
Healing may not be beautiful in the moment, but the life it opens is.

CHAPTER THREE

Peace

Silent Days and Zero Notifications

Silent days and zero notifications are not signs of emptiness, they are sacred spaces where your spirit breathes and recalibrates.

In a world addicted to noise and constant stimulation, choosing stillness is a radical act of self-preservation. It's in these quiet stretches of time, away from the pings and pulls of external validation, that your energy finds its way back home. You remember who you are when no one is watching, and what truly matters when no one is interrupting.

When the space between moments becomes something to feel, instead of to fill, your thoughts become your own again.

Protecting your peace isn't selfish, it's survival. Sometimes the loudest form of self-love is silence.

Vessel of Healing

Hurt people often hurt others, not out of malice, but because their own wounds distort how they see the world.

Pain, when left unaddressed, can spill over, shaping actions and relationships in ways that perpetuate cycles of suffering.

When someone hurts you, revenge may promise satisfaction, but its sweetness is an illusion; in truth, it is bitter and binds us more deeply to the very pain we wish to escape. By striking back, we extend the life of the wound rather than begin its healing. Forgiveness, on the other hand, is not weakness, it's a powerful choice to disrupt the cycle. When people take the time to confront their pain, to forgive others and themselves, they begin to break these patterns.

True strength is revealed not in the impulse for revenge, but in the quiet, courageous act of compassion toward those who have caused us pain. When we choose kindness over anger, we become vessels of healing, not just for ourselves, but for the ones who wounded us.

In offering grace instead of retaliation, we break the cycle of hurt and invite something sacred: the possibility of redemption, of transformation.

Helping someone heal, even when they've hurt us, is not about forgetting the pain but transcending it. It's the recognition that wounded people often wound others, and by choosing empathy, we plant the seeds of understanding where bitterness could have grown.

This path is not easy, but it is profoundly human and intensely healing.

Healed people, having walked through the fire and emerged stronger, offer compassion instead of judgment, understanding instead of retaliation. They become sources of peace and restoration, proving that while pain can be contagious, so can healing, and forgiveness is often the bridge between the two.

Honouring My Worth

Choosing myself means honouring my own worth, even when it feels uncomfortable or unfamiliar. It's the quiet revolution of setting boundaries, walking away from what diminishes me, and no longer shrinking to fit spaces I've outgrown.

It's not selfish, it's survival.

It's the realisation that my peace, growth, and joy are not optional, but necessary. Choosing myself is choosing to heal, to rest, to grow, and to show up for life on my own terms. It's understanding that no one is coming to rescue me and that's okay.

I am my own saviour. I am the one who picks myself up, speaks truth to my fears, and keeps moving forward. This kind of strength is built, not given and in choosing myself, I finally begin to feel free.

To choose compassion for yourself, in a world that can be cruel, to stay soft in the face of hardness, requires courage far beyond what force or anger can offer. Having the wisdom to respond, not react, and the self-respect to walk away when needed, is the quiet power of knowing who you are and not needing to prove or justify yourself.

Love yourself back to whole

Love yourself not in loud applause,
but in the quiet, unseen ways
in the breath you take
when the world feels too heavy,
in the moment you choose rest
instead of running.

Love the pieces
you once cast aside,
the ones too tender,
too wild, too much
gather them gently.
Call them sacred.

Let the scars speak
without shame,
let the silence
be a song
that sings you back
to softness.

You don't need to bloom overnight,
even roots take time to stretch
beneath the weight of becoming,
let that be enough.
You are not a project.
You are a place.

A home.
A wholeness
waiting to remember itself.
Love yourself
not to fix what's broken,
but to honour what's still here.
Still breathing.
Still beautiful.
Still *you*.

The gentle becoming

It didn't happen all at once.
Peace didn't crash through my door,
it arrived softly,
like sunlight finding its way
through the smallest crack in the curtain.
Some days, it was only a flicker,
a breath that didn't hurt,
a morning where the sky
didn't feel so heavy.
Other days, it was the sound
of my own laughter
startling me awake,
proof that joy still lived here.
I stopped asking myself
when I would be 'done' healing.
I started noticing
how my hands unclenched,
how my shoulders softened,
how I could sit in silence
without fearing what I'd hear.
The storms still come,
but they no longer take the whole sky.
I am learning to stand in the rain
without losing my ground.
And slowly,
with patience, with kindness,
with the quiet work

no one else can see,
I am becoming a place
where my own heart
feels safe to rest.

After Survival

There was a time when my body was a fortress, my mind a watchtower. Every sound was a possible threat, every choice a calculation. My breath never sank deep into my lungs, it lived high in my chest, ready to be snatched away at a moment's notice.

Survival mode is an unforgiving place. It doesn't care about beauty or joy. It asks only: *"Are you safe? Are you prepared? Can you endure?"*

And so, I endured. I built walls of vigilance and lit fires of determination. I became so good at enduring that I forgot what living felt like. Now, slowly, the ground beneath me feels less like quicksand. I notice how the air smells different when you aren't scanning for danger, it's softer somehow, less metallic.

The silence no longer feels like the pause before something bad happens; it feels like a quiet gift, a space to breathe in without flinching. I'm learning to want more than safety. Safety is the floor, not the ceiling. I want connection without suspicion, joy without the tight knot in my stomach, rest without guilt.

I want to be present enough to taste my coffee instead of gulping it like fuel.
I want to speak without rehearsing my sentences in case they're used against me.

The strangest part of leaving survival mode is that it doesn't happen all at once. My body still twitches with old reflexes. Sometimes the shadows still look like threats. But I remind myself: '*That was then. This is now.*'

It's not about forgetting the battles I fought, they shaped me. But I'm no longer a soldier in an endless war.

I'm a gardener now. My hands still remember how to build walls, but they're learning how to plant flowers instead.

And so, each day, I try to live as if I am safe, because I am. And maybe that is the bravest thing I've ever done.

Home to Self

Emerging from the darkness of pain is not a sudden awakening, but a slow and trembling ascent, a quiet, courageous crawl toward the light after being lost in the depths of despair. In that darkness, every breath feels heavy, every step uncertain, and the silence echoes with memories we wish we could forget.

Healing begins in the smallest of moments: a tear finally shed, a truth finally spoken, a glimpse of hope where there was once only numbness. As we rise, we begin to feel warmth again, subtle, unfamiliar, yet undeniable. The light does not erase the past, but it softens its edges, reminding us that we are not broken beyond repair.

I am becoming. With every scar, I carry a testament to my survival, and in that truth,
I discover the most sacred kind of strength, the kind that is born not from avoiding the darkness, but from walking through it and still choosing to stand in the light.

As the light grows steadier, something within begins to settle, like a storm that has finally passed, leaving behind a tender, quiet stillness. The pieces once thought lost begin to fit together in new, beautiful ways, not despite the cracks, but because of them.

There is a sense of wholeness, not perfection, but truth. A feeling of being home, not in a place, but in oneself.

The battle is not forgotten, but it no longer defines the present; it becomes part of a larger story, one of resilience, rebirth, and grace. Peace doesn't shout; it whispers, gently grounding the soul.

In the stillness, there is finally room to breathe, to dream, to love again. To feel safe within your own skin, and to know, with quiet certainty, you have returned to yourself.

Resurrection

There comes a time in a woman's life when the quiet ache of conformity becomes louder than the praise it once brought, and she begins to hear the voice within her rise above the noise of expectation. In that sacred, often storm-wrapped moment, she chooses herself, not as the world defines her, but as she truly is.

She lays down the armour forged by years of "shoulds" and "musts," and walks away from the roles she was told would complete her. No longer seeking permission to exist in her fullness, she removes the shackles of societal expectation one link at a time, until the weight of duty gives way to the lightness of freedom. This is not rebellion, it is resurrection.
A return to the wild, wise knowing that she was always enough, just as she is.

To walk the path of self-acceptance is to finally exhale after holding your breath for years. It is a quiet, radical act of coming home to yourself, without apology, without shame.
The mental freedom it brings is not loud or boastful, but steady and profound, like sunlight seeping through the cracks of long-closed windows. No longer measuring worth by comparison or approval, a woman begins to live in alignment with her own rhythm, her own truth.

The constant inner battles fought in mirrors, in conversations, in silences begin to still. In their place blooms a deep, sustaining peace: the kind that doesn't waver with others' opinions, because it is rooted in knowing.

To be able to accept oneself is to reclaim power, to love without condition, and to realise that freedom was never out there, it was always waiting within.

Waves of peace

Peace an overwhelming calm,
my restless mind begins to still.
Waves of fear and overthinking
ebb and flow, but now I will
find space to breathe, to live, to let go,
to accept the tides within.
The storm may stir, but I have learned
to meet it with quiet skin.
Peace, not silence, but a dance—
a gentle, steady flow,
where thinking comes, then drifts away,
and calm begins to grow.

I remember now

There is a stillness in me tonight
a sacred hush after years of noise,
a space I carved with quiet rebellion
and the aching need to *return*.

I remember now.
Not the version of me dressed in approval,
smiling through silences,
shrinking into the corners of other people's comfort
but the *real* me,
the one who speaks in firelight and instinct,
who blooms wildly without apology.

I no longer bend to be understood.
I no longer barter my peace for belonging.
I no longer wear the names they gave me
when I've always had my own.

This is what it means to come home.
To choose yourself in the still morning,
to walk away without explanation,
to say *yes* only when your soul echoes it back.
I am not here to fit in
I am here to *live*.
On my terms.
In my time.
Rooted in the truth I buried
under years of being "good."

Let the world keep spinning.
I will move at the rhythm of my own breath.
In this rhythm,
I am free.
I remember now.
And I will not forget again.

Epilogue: What Now?

If you've made it to the final page of *In My Healing Era*, then you've done more than just read a book, you've walked beside me. You've stood in the ruins of heartbreak and loss, felt the sting of old wounds reopening, and held space for the parts of me…and maybe parts of yourself that weren't always easy to face. You've witnessed the tender, tangled journey of what it means to heal: the aching, the unravelling, the small, steady blooms of hope that grew from the cracks.

You've seen how healing is far from neat. It doesn't follow a map or a straight line. It doubles back, loops around, knocks the wind out of us just when we think we're finally standing tall. But it also holds us in ways we never expected, in softness, in strength, in small mercies and unexpected joy. Healing is both the storm and the stillness that follows. It's grief and grace, truth and transformation. It's both the breaking and the becoming.

So… what now?
Now, we keep going.

The journey doesn't end here — not with the last poem, not with the final tear, not even with the deepest revelation. Healing isn't something you finish. It's something you live. It lingers in the quiet moments: in the ordinary rhythms of our days, in the way our breath returns to us after a panic, in the silence after saying goodbye to something, or someone we once thought we couldn't live without. It shows up when we least expect it, and sometimes when we're not even looking for it. It rises like a tide, slow and steady, washing over us until we realise we've softened.

Healing stretches us. It shapes us. It doesn't always feel good. Sometimes it feels like starting over, like peeling back layers we thought we'd already shed. But maybe that's the whole point. Maybe healing isn't about going back to who we were. Maybe it's about becoming someone new, someone more honest, more open, more rooted in who they are. Someone who chooses peace, even when chaos is familiar. Someone who honours their scars, but doesn't let them define the rest of their story.

For me, what's next looks like setting boundaries that protect my peace, even when it's hard, even when it costs me comfort or approval. It looks like speaking my truth, even when my voice shakes. It looks like trusting my intuition, even when logic tells me otherwise. It means leaning into the kind of healing that doesn't always come dressed as a grand ceremony or a curated retreat. Sometimes, the most powerful healing shows up in the quietest places: in the pages of my journal, in long walks through golden light, in slow mornings with coffee and a book, in soul-deep conversations with people who truly see me. It's in laughter shared over a great meal, or the solitude that doesn't feel lonely. It's in honest conversations, in allowing rest without guilt, in saying no without apology I'm learning to honour the sacred in the simple. I'm learning to see the divine in the ordinary. I'm learning that healing doesn't have to be loud to be powerful. That growth can happen even when no one is watching. That there's courage in simply continuing. In getting up each day and meeting yourself exactly where you are.

You might return to these pages when you need a reminder. Or maybe you'll write your own. Because healing isn't only found in poems and journal entries, it's found in how we choose to live, how we speak to ourselves, how we hold space for others, and how we keep showing up. It lives in the way we talk to ourselves in the mirror. In the way we forgive ourselves for who we used to be. In the way we hold space for others without shrinking ourselves. It's in how we show up for our joy, for our pain, and for the messy, beautiful in-between.

So here is your invitation:

Carry your peace forward. Let your pain become part of your power. Let it shape you, not shatter you. Let it teach you softness *and* strength. Know that healing is not a finish line to cross, but a way of living, a daily choice to meet yourself with grace and compassion, again and again and again.

You are still healing, yes — but you are also already whole.
You are not broken; you are becoming.
You are not behind; you are exactly where you need to be.
And in that paradox of healing and wholeness, of growing and grounding, lives your greatest power.
So keep going.
The story isn't over.
In fact, you're just getting started.
And so am I.
We're in this together; not just in the pain, but in the rising.

J x

In My Healing Era, inspired by the powerful words of Sarah Blondin, Donna Ashworth, Dr Shefali Tsabary and the following quotes....

1. *"Healing is not a destination. It is a journey."*
   – Unknown

2. *"I am not what happened to me, I am what I choose to become."*
   – Carl Jung

3. *"You do not just wake up and become the butterfly—growth is a process."*
   – Rupi Kaur

4. *"Healing is an art. It takes time, it takes practice. It takes love."*
   – Maza Dohta

5. *"There is no deadline for healing. You don't have to feel ashamed for taking longer than you thought you would."*
   – Unknown

6. *"You are not a mess. You are a feeling person in a messy world."*
   – Glennon Doyle

7. *"Healing is a matter of time, but it is sometimes also a matter of opportunity."*
   — Hippocrates

8. *"The wound is the place where the Light enters you."*
   — Rumi

9. *"Healing doesn't mean the damage never existed. It means the damage no longer controls your life."*

— Akshay Dubey (often quoted anonymous

10. *"Healing takes courage, and we all have courage, even if we have to dig a little to find it."*

— Tori Amos

Printed in Dunstable, United Kingdom

81261934R00040